the facts about
ELECTRICITY

Rebecca Hunter

FRANKLIN WATTS
LONDON•SYDNEY

© Franklin Watts 2003

First published in 2003 by
Franklin Watts
96 Leonard Street
London
EC2A 4XD

Franklin Watts Australia
45-51 Huntley Street
Alexandria
NSW 2015

ISBN: 0-7496-4879-1

A CIP catalogue record for this book is available from
the British Library

Printed in Hong Kong/China
Planning and production by Discovery Books Limited
Editor: Rebecca Hunter
Design: Keith Williams
Consultant: Jeremy Bloomfield
Illustrations: Stefan Chabluk

Photographs:
British Nuclear Fuels: page 18; **Corbis:** cover, page 4, 6,
10 left, 16, 20 left, 21, 23 top; **Discovery Picture Library:**
page 7, 8 left, 10, 12, 14, 26 bottom; **Edison Mission
Energy:** page 21, 28; **Moor Park School:** page 29;
National Grid: page 12; **Oxford Scientific Films:** page 5
(Robin Bush), 20 right (Ronald Toms), 22 (David M Dennis),
24 (Warren Faidley), 27 (Max Gibbs); **Phillips:** page 9;
Science Photo Library: page 8 right (Martin Riedl), 10 right
(Chris Knapton), 13 and 19 (Martin Bond), 23 bottom (G
Brad Lewis), 26 top (Peter Scoones), 28 (Hencoup
Enterprises).

ELECTRICITY

Contents

4 Electricity around us

6 Mains electricity

8 Cells and batteries

10 Electrical circuits

12 Conductors and insulators

14 Changing circuits

16 Circuit diagrams

18 Making electricity

20 Clean electricity

22 Using electricity

24 Static electricity

26 Electric animals

28 Electronic communications

30 Glossary

31 Further information

32 Index

Words in **bold** appear in the glossary on page 30.

Electricity around us

Electricity is a form of **energy**. It is very useful because it can be changed easily into other forms of energy.

Electricity has completely transformed the way people live. Only 150 years ago there were no electrical machines; now we can't imagine life without them. Electrical devices are all around us.

You can do it...

Count how many electrical devices you use in your day. Some are listed here, but there are many more. As a start, you could begin by counting how many electric machines you have in your house.

Electricity in your life

Think about how many times you use electricity every day. In the morning you may be woken by an electric alarm clock. You may turn on the radio and the lights – both are powered by electricity. For breakfast you might make a cup of tea, boiling the water in an electric kettle, and have some toast that has been made in an electric toaster. As you leave for school, you might listen to your personal stereo. The cars, lorries and buses on the road all have electric **batteries**.

◄ We rely on electricity to provide us with many forms of entertainment.

▲ Auckland, New Zealand, at night.
Cities use huge amounts of electricity.

Schools, offices, shops and factories are also powered by electricity. They contain electrical devices such as telephones, cash tills and computers. At the end of the day you might watch television, or eat a meal cooked on an electric cooker.

Electricity plays an important part in our lives. We cannot see it – but we can see what it does.

key facts

- Electricity is a form of energy.
- Electricity is used to power many machines.
- Without electricity our lives would be very different.

Mains electricity

The electricity we use in the home and at work is called mains, or current, electricity.

Mains electricity reaches your home through a cable. This is connected to a **power station** which may be many kilometres away. Mains electricity flows through cables in a similar way to water flowing through a hose. We call this flow an electric current. **Current electricity** is very easy to use because it can be sent along cables to wherever it is needed.

Electricity in the house

Once the electricity cable reaches your house a set of wires carries it through the walls, under the floors and around the ceilings. One set of cables carries electricity for the lights. Switches on the wall let you turn each light on and off.

▶ Electricity is carried across the countryside in cables which are strung between pylons.

Another set of wires goes to sockets in the wall. You can connect electrical machines to these sockets using a plug with metal pins. When you push the pins into the socket and switch it on, electricity flows through the plug and along the wire to the machine.

Mains electricity can be very dangerous. If it flows through your body it will give you an electric shock which could kill you.

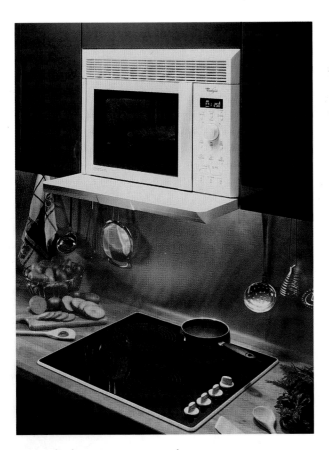

▲ Both this stove top and microwave oven run on electricity. They have cables and plugs which connect to the mains electricity in the house.

Safety

Follow these rules to stay safe from electricity:
- Never touch the bare metal of electrical wires. The wires should always be covered in plastic.
- Electric sockets are for plugs only. NEVER stick anything else into a socket.
- Do not use electric machines near water.
- Do not touch light switches or plugs with wet hands.

Cells and batteries

Mains electricity is not the only kind of electricity. We can also get electricity from **cells** or batteries.

Mobile phones, radios, calculators, clocks and torches only need a small amount of electricity. They get it from a cell filled with **chemicals**. When these chemicals **react** with each other they produce a small electric current.

Batteries

A battery is a group of cells that are joined together. The cells are placed next to each other in a casing.

▶ Many of the electrical items we use today are powered by batteries. This girl is talking on a cordless phone which contains a battery.

▲ Batteries for a torch or radio.

Voltage

The first battery was invented in 1800 by an Italian count, Alessandro Volta. The **volt**, the unit for measuring electric force, is named after him. The power of a cell or battery is measured in volts. A small cell may give 1.5 volts of electricity. Cells can be connected together into batteries to provide more electricity. A small torch may use two 1.5-volt cells, so it has 3 volts. A radio may use a 9-volt battery which contains six 1.5-volt cells.

Uses of batteries

Small batteries are a much safer way to get electricity than mains electricity. They supply much less power and are not dangerous. Most batteries are small and light. This means the machines they power can be easily carried around. A personal stereo that had to be plugged into the wall would not be nearly as much fun!

Batteries come in many sizes. Watches and calculators use tiny, button-sized batteries. Torches and toys use batteries that are a few centimetres long. Cars use large, heavy batteries to start their engines.

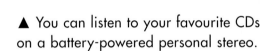

▲ You can listen to your favourite CDs on a battery-powered personal stereo.

Positive and negative

A battery has a positive and a negative terminal. In order to make the electricity flow, the terminals need to be joined together in a **circuit**.

key facts

- Electricity can be obtained from batteries.

- A battery is made up of a number of cells.

- The power of a battery is measured in volts.

Electrical circuits

A circuit is a circle that electricity can flow around.
Electricity can only flow if the circuit is complete.

Several things are needed to make up an electrical circuit: a supply of electricity, connectors (to join the different parts together) and at least one **component** (something that uses electricity).

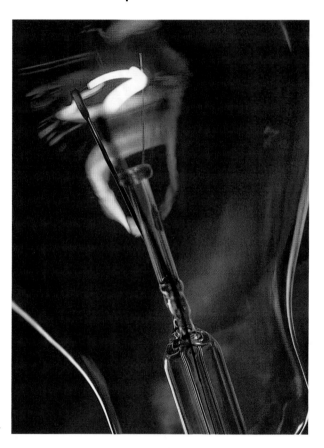

▲ A close-up view of a light bulb. When it is connected to an electrical circuit, the filament glows brightly.

▲ All the lights on this Christmas tree are connected in a circuit.

Every electrical circuit must get electricity from somewhere. In a simple circuit the electricity comes from a battery. You can join two or more batteries together to get more power. Metal wires connect all the parts of a circuit. They allow electricity to flow from one component to the next.

Circuit components

The circuit also needs something to use the electricity and show that the circuit is working. This could be a motor, a buzzer or a light bulb. The wire inside a light bulb is called a filament, and is very thin. When electricity passes through it, the filament glows.

Battery (supply of electricity)

Wire connector

Light bulb (component)

You can do it...

Make a simple circuit. You will need a battery in a battery holder, a light bulb in a light bulb holder, and two wires. Attach a wire to each end of the battery holder, and then attach the wires to each side of the light bulb holder. If the circuit is complete, the light bulb will light up. Does your bulb light up? What happens if you break the circuit?

key facts

○ Electricity can only flow around a circuit.

○ A simple circuit needs a battery, two wires and a light bulb.

○ If the circuit is broken, the electricity will not flow.

Conductors and insulators

Electricity can pass through some materials but not through others. Materials that electricity can pass through are called **conductors**. Those that stop electricity passing through are called **insulators**.

Conductors

All metals conduct electricity. That is why we use metal wires in circuits. Some metals are better conductors than others. Copper, aluminium, gold and silver are all very good conductors. Electrical wire is usually made of copper, because it is cheap and easily available. Gold and silver are even better conductors, but it would be much too expensive to make wires out of them!

Insulators

Many materials do not conduct electricity. If something does not conduct electricity, it is called an insulator. Plastic, rubber, wood and glass are all good insulators. All electrical wires should be insulated with a plastic coating to protect people from electric shocks.

▶ Glass discs are used as insulators to hold power cables on electricity pylons. Thick glass is a very good insulator; it is also strong, durable and weatherproof.

▼ Plastic is an insulator. This plastic ruler will not conduct electricity and so the light bulb will not glow.

Test materials to see if they are conductors or insulators. Make up a simple circuit with three wires and leave a gap between two of them, as shown in the diagrams. Put the material to be tested in the gap and attach the two wires to it. If the material is a conductor of electricity the bulb will light up. If the material is an insulator the bulb will not glow.

▼ If a metal object is used to connect the circuit, the light bulb glows. This shows the object is a conductor of electricity.

key facts

- Conductors are materials that allow electricity to pass through them.

- Insulators do not allow electricity to pass through them.

- All metals are conductors of electricity.

- Plastic, rubber, wood and glass are good insulators.

Changing circuits

Several components can be added to a simple circuit to make it do more things or to control the flow of electricity.

Switches

Most circuits have a switch. A switch allows you to control the flow of electricity in a circuit by switching it off. This is convenient and saves money since most electric machines do not need to be on all the time.

You can add a switch to a simple circuit using a paper clip. This is done by cutting one of the wires and then screwing a paper clip on to a piece of wood.

▼ Switches around the house enable you turn the lights on and off.

Attach the two ends of the wire to the screws underneath the paper clip, as shown in the diagram below. By moving the paper clip you can either join the wires and allow the electricity to flow, or break the circuit and stop the electricity.

▲ Switch on: light bulb glows.

▲ Switch off: light bulb does not glow.

Adding more batteries

What would you expect to happen if you added more batteries to your circuit? When another battery is added to the circuit, more electricity flows through so the light in the bulb is brighter. But take care not to add too many batteries or the bulb will 'blow': the filament will burn out and break.

▲ With two light bulbs, each bulb glows more faintly.

Adding more components

Light bulbs are the components in the simple circuits shown here, but you can also use others such as motors or buzzers.

▲ With two batteries, the light bulb glows brightly.

Adding more light bulbs

When you add more light bulbs to a simple circuit, the bulbs are dimmer because the same amount of electricity is having to light up more bulbs. If you want to put more components into a circuit, you will need to add more batteries, too.

key facts

- Switches control the supply of electricity in a circuit.

- The more bulbs you add to a simple circuit, the dimmer each will be.

- Circuits can be changed by adding more batteries or more components.

Circuit diagrams

A **circuit diagram** is a map or plan of a circuit. Each of the components in the circuit has a **symbol** to represent it.

A circuit diagram shows whether or not a circuit will work. Scientists use circuit diagrams in order to work out what will happen when a circuit is changed.

Because it would be difficult each time to draw all the components in a circuit, scientists use symbols to represent them.

▶ A table showing the components in a circuit, and the symbols for them used in a circuit diagram.

▼ Imagine what the circuit diagram for this department store would look like!

Component	Symbol
battery	
two batteries	
bulb	
buzzer	
motor	
switch – off	
switch – on	

▲ This circuit diagram represents the simple circuit shown on page 11.

Can you tell which of the diagrams below represents the circuit shown on the right? (You will find the answer on page 30.)

1

2

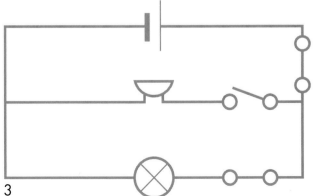

3

key facts

- Circuits can be drawn as diagrams.

- Each component of a circuit has a symbol.

- You can tell if a circuit will work by looking at its circuit diagram.

Making electricity

If a **magnet** is spun near a coil of wire, electricity is produced in the wire. This is how most electricity is made.

The dynamo

A dynamo changes movement energy into electrical energy. A bicycle dynamo has a small wheel that touches the wall of the bicycle tyre. As the tyre turns, the dynamo wheel is also turned. Inside the dynamo the wheel is attached to a magnet. When the magnet spins it produces an electric current in a coil of wire. It makes enough electricity to power the lights on the bicycle.

A dynamo

Dynamo wheel

Bicycle tyre

Magnet
Wire coil

Cable which carries electricity to the lamp

Generators

Most of the electricity we use is generated in power stations. It is made by powerful machines called **generators**.

◄ The interior of a power station. Inside the large blue containers, turbines turn and generate the electricity.

▼ A coal-fired power station. What looks like black smoke belching out from the towers is in fact harmless steam.

A generator is like a very large dynamo. Inside the power station, water is heated to boiling point and turned into steam. The steam drives **turbines** which rotate very quickly to produce electricity. The output of a power station is 400,000 volts.

The electricity is carried around the country by cables, often strung between pylons or buried underground. Devices called transformers reduce the voltage in stages to provide the level of supply required by various customers. The electricity used in shops, homes and offices is 230 volts. That used by industry is 11,000 volts.

Fossil fuels

Most power stations burn fuels such as coal, oil or natural gas. These are called **fossil fuels** because they are the remains of long-dead plants and animals. They are useful, high-energy fuels, but when they are burned they release a gas called carbon dioxide that **pollutes** the air.

Another problem with fossil fuels is that they are being used up quickly. At the present rate, the world's supply will run out in about 250 years. That is why it is important to find new ways of making cleaner electricity.

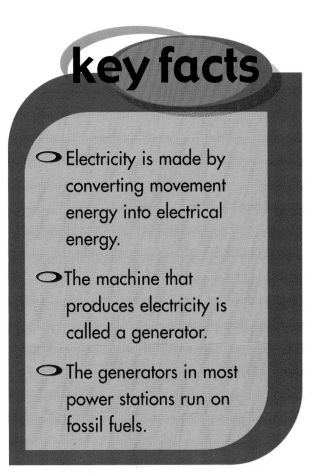

key facts

- Electricity is made by converting movement energy into electrical energy.

- The machine that produces electricity is called a generator.

- The generators in most power stations run on fossil fuels.

Clean electricity

There are other ways of generating electricity. Many of these do not pollute the **environment** and are also **renewable**, which means they will not run out.

Electricity can be made using the power of the wind, the tides, the Sun and water. These methods are generally much less harmful to the environment than burning fossil fuels.

Solar power

The Earth gets a huge amount of energy from the Sun. **Solar energy** is non-polluting and renewable. Solar cells convert sunlight (solar energy) into electricity. Solar cells are found in solar-powered calculators, radio beacons and, in remote parts of the world, even telephone links.

◄ One of the big advantages of solar energy is that it can provide instant electricity in very remote places. Here, a solar-powered phone is being used in an isolated area of the USA.

Solar cells are also used in space satellites, and navigation buoys at sea. Some domestic homes now have solar panels on their roofs which provide them with 'free' electricity.

Wind power

Wind power is another clean source of energy. Windmills have been used to grind corn and pump water for many centuries. Today wind 'farms' have hundreds of wind turbines which turn in the wind and generate electricity.

▼ These wind turbines are part of a wind farm near Palm Springs, California, USA.

◀ The Hoover Dam HEP station is built across the Colorado River in Nevada, USA.

Geothermal energy is heat energy that is stored in the hot, molten rock deep underground. About 20 countries use geothermal energy as a source of heat or to generate electricity.

Tidal power is produced by holding back sea water at high tide and then letting it flow out through turbines at low tide. A tidal power station at La Rance in France produces enough electricity for a city of 300,000 people.

key facts

- Solar energy is one way of producing cleaner electricity.

- Hydroelectric power provides one-fifth of the world's electricity.

- Wind, sea tides and geothermal heat can also be used to make electricity.

Other energy sources

Other clean sources of energy include hydroelectric power, tidal power and geothermal energy. About 20 per cent of the world's energy comes from hydroelectric power (or HEP). This is power created by the movement of water.

In an HEP station, a river is dammed to create a lake. When the water is allowed to flow through the dam, a generator changes the water's movement energy into electrical energy.

Using electricity

When we use electricity, we are converting electrical energy into other forms of energy: heat, light, sound or movement.

Heat and light

One of the main ways we use electrical energy is to convert it into heat energy. When electricity is passed through a wire, the wire gets hot. In toasters and electric heaters, you can see how the wire glows red with heat.

Electricity produces light in just the same way. Light bulbs contain a thin wire, or filament, made of a metal called tungsten. When electricity is passed through the filament it glows white-hot and so gives out light. The light bulb is filled with the gas argon, which stops the tungsten wire from burning up. Eventually the filament becomes weak and snaps. Then the bulb 'blows' and has to be replaced.

You can do it...

Look at a clear light bulb using a magnifying glass. Can you see how the tungsten filament is tightly coiled? The more coils there are, the brighter the light. The power of a light bulb is measured in watts (W). Household bulbs range between 25W (the dimmest) and 150W (the brightest). The power of the bulb is printed on the glass.

▲ On its own an electric guitar is quite quiet. The sounds are changed into electrical signals and made louder in an **amplifier**.

Sound

Televisions, stereos, radios and computers all use electricity to produce sound. Today, one person can create the sound of a whole orchestra using just an electric keyboard and a computer.

Movement

Electric motors power many different machines. Washing machines, food processors and lawn mowers are all motors that turn electricity into movement. Cars have electric motors to help them start and to work the windscreen wipers. Research is being done to build cars that use only electricity, but at the moment they need enormous batteries to supply enough power for even a short journey.

key facts

- Electrical energy can be converted into heat, light, sound and movement energy.

- Both heat and light are created by passing electricity through a wire.

- Scientists and inventors are working to build an electric car that can travel long distances.

◄ This prototype car is powered by electricity. It has batteries which can be charged, and solar panels on its roof.

Static electricity

There is another kind of electricity called **static electricity**. Unlike current electricity, static electricity does not flow.

Making static electricity

Static electricity is caused by a build-up of electrical charges. There are two types of electrical charge: a positive charge and a negative charge. It is easy to see this in practice. If you rub a balloon against a woollen sweater it becomes charged with electricity. The balloon gets a negative electric charge, while your sweater has a positive charge. If you let go of the balloon it will stay attached to the sweater: this is because two differently charged objects are attracted to each other.

Thunderstorms

We can also see static electricity at work during a thunderstorm. Inside the storm clouds pieces of ice and hail rub together and become charged with electricity. This is discharged as a flash of lightning.

Although we may only experience a thunderstorm a few times each year, the Earth is actually being struck by lightning over 100 times a second!

▼ A dramatic lightning storm in Arizona, USA.

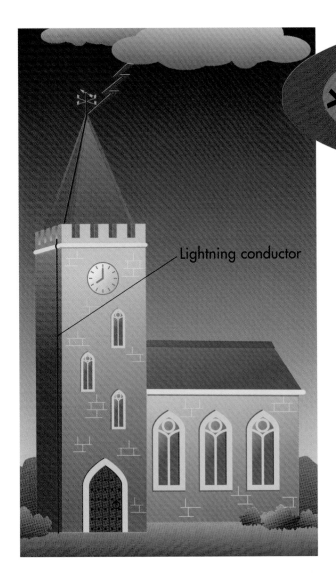

Lightning conductor

See how like charges repel each other. Tie some cotton thread on to two balloons and hang them together on a stick. Rub each balloon in turn on the same woollen sweater. What happens? Both balloons have the same static charge so they push each other away.

key facts

- Static electricity does not flow like current electricity.

- Static electricity is caused by a build-up of electric charges.

- Lightning is caused by static electricity.

- Opposite charges attract each other, while like charges repel.

If the charges in the thunderstorm cloud are strong enough, the lightning can force a path through the air to the ground. Tall buildings, trees and even people may be struck by the charge, which can carry up to 100 million volts of electricity. Many tall buildings such as churches have a metal rod on the roof called a lightning conductor. This is connected to the ground. If lightning does strike, the conductor carries the charge harmlessly to the ground.

Electric animals

Electricity is not just seen in lightning or generated in power stations. It can also be produced by animals.

Nervous systems

Our bodies are run by electricity. Like all animals, we have a brain, which controls different parts of our body by receiving and sending electrical **impulses**, or signals, through our nerves. Every time we touch something an electrical signal is sent through our nervous system to our brain.

▼ When you touch a cat, an electrical signal is sent to your brain. The brain tells you that the cat's fur is soft and pleasant to stroke.

▲ The Australian duck-billed platypus closes its ears and eyes when it dives. It searches for food under water using electrical signals, which it senses with its very sensitive bill.

Our brain then tells us what response to make. This all happens at very high speed. When you pick up a pan that is too hot, your brain tells you immediately to drop it.

The amount of electrical charge used in our bodies is very small, but some animals can make enough electricity to stun or even kill other animals.

The knife-fish

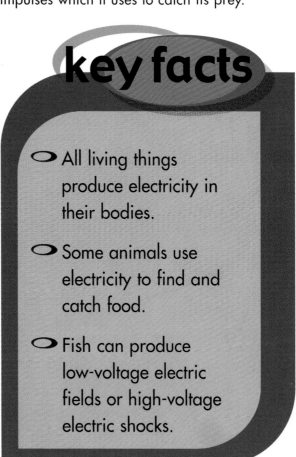

The Amazon knife-fish is a very odd-looking fish. It is about 20 cm long and has only one fin that runs all the way along the underside of its body. Above this fin, buried under its skin, is a line of **organs** which give out low-voltage electrical impulses. These create an area called an electric field. The knife-fish can sense any small fish that swims into this electric field and so is able to catch it easily.

▲ The knife-fish produces low-voltage electrical impulses which it uses to catch its prey.

The electric eel

The South American electric eel can produce a massive electric shock of up to 600 volts that will kill or stun any fish nearby. If you picked one up without wearing rubber gloves or boots, the shock would be enough to throw you flat on your back. In some cases, horses standing in shallow water have been knocked over by the electricity produced by electric eels.

key facts

- All living things produce electricity in their bodies.

- Some animals use electricity to find and catch food.

- Fish can produce low-voltage electric fields or high-voltage electric shocks.

Electronic communications

Today, electricity makes it possible for us not just to talk to someone on the other side of the world, but to send them messages and pictures instantly.

Electronic equipment changes sounds and pictures into electricity and sends them at amazing speed over thousands of kilometres. When they reach their destination they are changed back into sounds and pictures by other electronic equipment. All electronic communication needs a device called a **transmitter** to send out the information, something to carry the signals, and a **receiver** to change the signals back into a form we can understand.

The telephone

The first telephone was built in 1876 by Alexander Graham Bell. Bell was a teacher of deaf people and was interested in trying to change speech into electrical signals that could be sent down a wire.

When you dial a number, the dialling tones pass along wires to your local telephone exchange. You will then be connected with an exchange in the area that you are calling. You may sometimes notice a slight delay when talking to someone overseas. This is because your call is going via a satellite in space! Huge dish-shaped aerials on the ground transmit the signals up to the satellite. The solar-powered satellite beams the signals back to an aerial in another part of the world.

▼ This satellite dish is part of NASA's Deep Space Network. It tracks and communicates with satellites and space-craft throughout the solar system.

▲ Most schools are now connected to the Internet, giving students access to vast quantities of information on almost every subject.

The Internet

One of the most important modern electronic communication devices is the Internet. The Internet is a world-wide network of computers connected by high-speed telephone links. Using the Internet, which is powered by electricity, it is now possible to get information on any subject almost instantly, from anywhere in the world.

key facts

○ Electricity is used in many forms of telecommunication.

○ Telephones, the Internet, radios, televisions and computers all need electricity in order to work.

Glossary

Amplifier A machine that increases the loudness of sounds.

Battery A battery stores electricity. It is made up of several cells.

Cell A container that holds chemicals that make electricity flow through a circuit.

Chemicals Substances that can be found naturally or manufactured.

Circuit diagram Plan of a circuit which uses symbols to show all the components in a circuit and how they are connected.

Circuit The circle containing wires, components and a battery, through which electricity flows.

Component A device in a circuit.

Conductor Something that allows electricity to flow through it easily.

Current electricity Electricity that flows through a wire or cable.

Energy What people, animals and machines need to give them the power to do work.

Environment The surroundings that make up the place where you live.

Fossil fuels Fossil fuels like coal, oil and natural gas are all obtained from the fossilised remains of plants and animals that lived millions of years ago.

Generator A machine at a power station that turns movement energy into electrical energy.

Impulse A short push or surge of energy.

Insulator Something that does not allow electricity to flow through it.

Magnet A piece of iron that attracts other pieces of iron or steel towards it.

Organs Internal parts of the body that perform different functions.

Pollute To make something dirty.

Power station A place that generates, or makes, electricity.

React To change because of something that has happened.

Receiver A device for receiving messages.

Renewable Describes something that you can always get more of.

Solar energy Energy from the Sun.

Static electricity Electricity which builds up on objects which are rubbed together. Static means 'not moving'.

Symbol A shape or picture that is used to represent something.

Transmitter A device that is used to transmit, or send, messages.

Turbine A machine that is made to rotate and drive a generator.

Volt/voltage The measure of the force of an electric current or the power of a battery.

Answer: Circuit diagram 3 represents the circuit shown on page 17.

Further information

Books

Light, Sound and Electricity,
Kirsteen Rogers, Usborne, 2001

Using Electricity,
Angela Royston,
Heinemann, 2001

Electricity: Where Does it Come From, Where
Does it Go?
Paul Humphrey,
Franklin Watts, 2000

Electricity,
Chris Ollenshaw,
A & C Black, 1999

Websites

Science Made Simple: Static Electricity
Easy to read description of the phenomenon,
plus fun projects you can do at home.
http://www.sciencemadesimple.com/static.html

Hydroelectric Power
Describes how water's mechanical energy is
turned into electricity.
From the National Renewable Energy Laboratory.
http://www.nrel.gov/lab/pao/hydroelectric.html

How do you make electricity?
Find out how by asking Earl!
http://www.yahooligans.com/content/ask_earl
/20020523.html

BrainPOP – Electricity
Watch cartoons, do quizzes and try experiments
about electricity and related topics such as
thunderstorms, batteries and other energy sources.
http://www.brainpop.com/science/electricity/

Electricity Online
Learn all about electricity, its applications, and
its history. Features experiments, activities and
an historical timeline.
http://library.thinkquest.org/28032/

Places to Visit

UK
The Science Museum
Exhibition Road, South Kensington,
London SW7 2DD

Museum of Science and Industry
Castlefield, Manchester M3 4FP

Glasgow Science Centre
50 Pacific Quay, Glasgow G51 1EA Scotland

Techniquest
Stuart Street, Cardiff CF10 5BW Wales

Australia
Australian Museum
6 College Street, Sydney NSW 2010

Scitech Discovery Centre
City West, Railway Parade, West Perth

Questacon
The National Science and Technology Centre
King Edward Terrace, Canberra ACT 2000

New Zealand
Otago Museum
Dunedin, New Zealand

Index

animals and electricity 26, 27

batteries 4, 8, 9, 11, 15

cables 6
cells 8, 9
circuit diagrams 16, 17
circuits 9, 10, 14, 15
communications 28, 29
components 10, 11, 14, 15, 16
computers 5, 29
conductors 12, 13
connectors 10, 11

duck-billed platypus 26
dynamo 18

electric cars 23
electric current 6, 8, 18
electric eel 27
electrical charges 24, 25, 26
electronics 28, 29
electric shocks 7, 12, 27
energy 4, 18, 22

filaments 10, 15, 22
fossil fuels 19

generating electricity 18, 19, 20, 21
generators 18, 19
geothermal energy 21

heat energy 22
hydroelectric power 21

insulators 12, 13
Internet 29

knife-fish 27

light bulbs 10, 11, 15, 22
light energy 5, 10, 22
lightning 24, 25
lightning conductors 25

machines 4, 7, 9
magnets 18
mains electricity 6, 7
metal 12, 13
movement energy 23

nervous systems 26

plastic 12, 13
plugs 7
pollution 19
power stations 6, 7, 18, 19
pylons 6, 19

renewable energy 20, 21

safety 7
sockets 7
satellites 28
solar power 20, 23
sound energy 23
static electricity 24, 25
switches 6, 14
symbols 16, 17

telephones 28
tidal power 21
transformers 19
transmitters 28
turbines 19

Volta, Alessandro 9
voltage 9, 19, 27

wind power 20
wires 6, 12